D1824465

STORIES
to
STRETCH
the
MIND
and
HEART

REV. DR. KAREN L. HOLGERSEN

BALBOA.PRESS
A DIVISION OF HAY HOUSE

Balboa Press books may be ordered through booksellers or by contacting:

Balboa Press
A Division of Hay House
1663 Liberty Drive
Bloomington, IN 47403
www.balboapress.com
844-682-1282

Because of the dynamic nature of the Internet, any web addresses or links contained in this book may have changed since publication and may no longer be valid. The views expressed in this work are solely those of the author and do not necessarily reflect the views of the publisher, and the publisher hereby disclaims any responsibility for them.

The author of this book does not dispense medical advice or prescribe the use of any technique as a form of treatment for physical, emotional, or medical problems without the advice of a physician, either directly or indirectly. The intent of the author is only to offer information of a general nature to help you in your quest for emotional and spiritual well-being. In the event you use any of the information in this book for yourself, which is your constitutional right, the author and the publisher assume no responsibility for your actions.

Any people depicted in stock imagery provided by Getty Images are models, and such images are being used for illustrative purposes only. Certain stock imagery © Getty Images.

Print information available on the last page.

ISBN: 978-1-9822-7417-7 (sc)
ISBN: 978-1-9822-7418-4 (hc)
ISBN: 978-1-9822-7416-0 (e)

Library of Congress Control Number: 2021918994

Balboa Press rev. date: 09/24/2021

DEDICATION

This book is dedicated to all my students,
with much love and respect.

CONTENTS

COURAGEOUS STORIES

PREFACE

The wise elders of a village or tribe would often teach the young through storytelling. Important cultural and societal norms would be passed on to the next generation through this method.

As an elementary school teacher, I discovered that my students really seemed to enjoy the storytelling experience. From time-to-time, I would tell true stories as a way of teaching lessons about life to my fourth and fifth grade students. They would often request a "Ms. Hogi/Dr. Hogi" story.

In my own humble way, I was trying to pass on wisdom to the next generation.

My students asked me to please put their favorite stories in a book. I promised I would write that book when I retired. I have now kept that promise.

Enjoy.

Dr. Hogi

INTRODUCTION

Although I like a balanced approach in literature, I have deliberately included more humorous stories than courageous stories.

Courage is incredibly important in our daily living experiences and sometimes, it is an act of courage to just get out of bed. I can certainly attest that it took much courage to face all the personal challenges in my life.

However, the one survival skill that has helped me the most was learning to laugh at myself and to learn to enjoy my own life story. With time, even the most horrendous experiences can be put into proper perspective.

I have almost passed into Spirit three times – once as a child, once as a teenager, and once as an adult. These close calls with death have given me the gift of clarity. I have learned that life can certainly be very complex. I have also learned that how one responds to the ups and downs is even more important than the life events themselves. For example, I can respond with gratitude for the joyous events in my life. I can even respond with understanding about the saddest events in my life because of the lessons learned from loss. As a natural optimist, I have also sought to see the sunny side of life – even during times of stormy weather.

I invite you to enjoy these true stories of courage and humor. It is my hope that you will find inspiration in the courageous stories, and you will laugh as much as you can at the humorous stories, as laughter lifts the spirits and is music to our soul.

I also invite you to reflect on a courageous or funny story you would like to share with a loved one. Please pass this story on as it adds meaning to your own life story and will be remembered by those who were lucky enough to hear it.

HUMOROUS STORIES

Humor is mankind's greatest blessing.
—Mark Twain

THE BUNNY TRAP

As a child, I wanted a pet bunny. My parents did not agree with this request. However, we had moved to the outskirts of a town and next to the house was a large field at the edge of the woods. From our house, my family could watch the bunnies come out of the blackberry brush cover and eat the grass at the edge of the field in the early morning.

Since I still wanted a pet bunny, I convinced my two younger brothers that it would be a great idea to make a bunny trap. Yes! We could catch a bunny in our bunny trap, and we could have a pet bunny. What could possibly go wrong?

Since my younger brothers and I would play for hours outside, we had plenty of time to develop this plan. This "catch the bunny" strategy was to dig holes where the grass met the woods, as it was hoped that the bunny would fall into the trap while feeding.

We worked so hard digging holes of different sizes next to the blackberry brush cover. After we finished digging the holes, we concluded that the bunny would see the hole(s) and jump right over them.

We decided to camouflage the holes by designing a cover for each hole. The bunny would step or jump on the cover and the weight would break the cover and the bunny would fall in the hole and be captured.

We constructed the covers by placing sticks in a crisscross pattern to provide support for the tufts of grass placed on the top. We gathered other natural materials to make the covers and the holes blend in.

How proud we were of ourselves! The bunny holes were camouflaged and finished. We were going to catch our bunny! We returned to our house and watched.

Unbeknownst to us, that was the summer day that our mother had chosen to pick blackberries to make blackberry pies. She had left the blackberry patch with her bowl full of blackberries.

Then, it happened.

We heard a scream and swearing. Our mother had stepped on one of the smaller holes. Oh, no! As she picked herself up, she still had the bowl of berries in her hand. However, that was to quickly change as the next thing we saw was our mother falling again. She had stepped on the larger bunny trap and had fallen in.

We had caught our mom instead of a bunny!

She was physically unhurt; however, all the blackberries had gone flying out of her bowl. We could hear her saying, "Wait until I get my hands on those kids!"

That did it. We knew we were in big trouble. We ran as we did not want to stay around and see what would happen next!

As a result, my brothers and I stayed in the woods all that day.

We never made another bunny trap.

LIFE LESSON: LIFE CAN BE FULL OF SURPRISES.

MY BEST MERMAID IMPRESSION

As a high school teenager, I dated a young man whose family had a motorboat. Living in northern California, we were blessed with several natural lakes, so the family used the boat for water skiing.

The young man asked his best buddy and me to go water skiing with him on one of the lakes. I have never skied before, and he had reassured me that I could learn this skill quickly. Afterall, I was quite an athlete at the time and had swum weekly in my elementary school program. I even had a lifeguard certificate. I was confident that this would be my new sport.

When we arrived at the lake, the guys launched the boat into the water. I watched both waterski as they demonstrated the proper technique. Then, it was my turn.

I stood on the pier with my water skis and life jacket on. The guys revved up the engine of the speedboat and holding on to the tow rope, I started to jettison forward. I went off the pier and hit the water. Unlike the guys, I had not kept my balance on top of the water but had sunk underneath and was completely submerged under the water.

The problem was that I continued to hold on to the tow rope! I was quickly propelled like a submarine under the surface although this submarine was attached to a rope.

Running out of air, it finally occurred to me to let go of the tow rope and swim to the surface. As I gasped for air, I realized that maybe this wasn't my new sport after all.

LIFE LESSON: SOMETIMES IT IS IMPORTANT TO LET GO.

AN AMERICAN IN PARIS

WHEN I WAS 17 YEARS OLD, I HAD THE HONOR OF BEING A PEOPLE-to-People Student Ambassador. I traveled to Europe during the summer of my rising senior year. The trip included ten countries in six weeks.

I had only been on an airplane once before, and now I was a part of the inaugural flight of the first passenger 747 flight from the United States to London, England. It was an amazing experience.

All the student ambassadors toured London after our arrival and stayed with different local families. After London, England, we were on our way to Paris, France. It had been a long day of travel and the first item of business (pardon the pun) upon arrival in our Parisian hotel was to locate the lavatory.

Unfortunately, the hotel room did not have a toilet as there was only one lavatory for each floor. I hurried to the lavatory in the hallway and went inside.

I immediately sat down on the first toilet and did my business. When I went to flush the toilet, however, there didn't seem to be a handle and to my dismay, the recently deposited poo pieces were now floating to the top of the toilet! I was horrified to watch the poo pieces float over the toilet and onto the bathroom floor.

I didn't know exactly why this was happening, however, now the floor was flooded with poo pieces that were floating. I grabbed some toilet paper and did my best to grab the floaters.

The toilet continued to flood, and I quickly returned to my room and called the front desk to report the problem.

I shared this story with some of the student ambassadors and they fell over laughing. They explained to me that I had gone to the bathroom in something called a bidet, and the bidet was for washing, and not for pooping.

Who knew?

This mistake was so embarrassing that I can still laugh about it to this day.

LIFE LESSON: THINGS CAN BE DIFFERENT FROM WHAT THEY APPEAR.

HI, HO, SILVER AWAY!

I WAS MARRIED THE FIRST TIME WHEN I WAS 18. MY LATE HUSBAND was a gentle soul who was very kind. We had become good friends when I was in high school, and he was in college as we met at a political event. I had wanted my late husband and I to be roommates as I began college and as he had graduated from college, he had started a job making less than $10,000 a year. I had planned on working part-time to help support myself.

He was my best friend and although *Three's Company* was a TV sitcom then, my conservative parents could not see their way to allowing their daughter to live with a man who was not her husband. Period.

Times have certainly changed over the decades, however, back then, no "good girl" would do such a thing. So, to appease my parents and to keep peace, we got married.

We ended up going on a honeymoon to Hawaii. We stayed on one of the less popular islands that had yet to become a tourist hot spot. We had the idea that it would be a more relaxing experience after all the hubbub of the wedding.

It certainly was remote. We watched large cranes plant full-sized palm trees and played near the ocean.

As part of the welcome package of activities, the hotel had suggested horse-back riding. My new husband wanted to go, and I explained to him that five years before, I had had a traumatic experience on a horse and now I was very afraid of them. I told him that horses could sense my extreme fear and wouldn't want me near them.

He reassured me that he would be nearby and would help me if anything untoward would occur.

I reluctantly agreed to go on the honeymoon horseback ride through the fields of sugar cane. It sounded so romantic.

We traveled to the site and all the riders took their mount. Clad in shorts and a summer top as it was very hot and humid, the tour guide helped me on the horse as I was the last to mount up. I was so scared.

That horse must have felt all that fear because before anyone could say or do anything else, that horse took off in a full gallop. Although I was in a saddle, I was too afraid to handle the horse. (I am sure my screaming didn't help.)

Just like in the western movies, where there is a runaway horse and a person is calling for help, and then, another person on a horse in full gallop rides quickly to stop the runaway horse by catching up to the horse and pulling on its reins – this was the scene of a movie that was now being reenacted in real life.

My new husband, and now my hero, rode his horse in a full gallop and eventually caught up to my runaway horse, leaned over, pulled on my horse's reins, and stopped my horse.

The shaken tour guide ordered his helper to get me another horse, and they chose for me the oldest and slowest horse they could find on the island. I was helped to mount this very old horse.

As the new horse could barely walk, I encouraged my husband to go ahead with the group as the rest of the group wanted to get going and have their scenic horse ride.

So, I let the horse just walk very slowly and do whatever it wanted as I did not want it to hurt me. This horse quickly figured out that it had won the lottery as it was not expected to catch up with the group or even care that it had a rider.

Thus, this horse would walk a few steps, then stop, and eat some sugar cane, then walk a few steps more, then stop, and eat some sugar cane. This continued for the entire ride.

Hours later, I made it back to the starting point and the horse was full of sugar cane. I had severe saddle burns as I had worn shorts instead of long pants.

I spent the next hours sitting in the ocean hoping the salt water would help heal my wounds in my inner thighs.

As I walked rather bow-legged back into the hotel, there was no cure for my embarrassment.

LIFE LESSON: HELP MAY COME WHEN YOU LEAST EXPECT IT.

SPLAT!

I grew up on the coast of northern California. There was a lot of rain, however, not frozen precipitation. As a result, you had to drive east toward the mountain ranges to see snow.

Therefore, I was middle-aged when I first got an opportunity to try snow-skiing. I had booked a mother-teenager bonding trip to a day-long snow skiing retreat event sponsored by the company I was working for at the time. We rode on the chartered bus and arrived at the ski resort ready to learn.

My teenage daughter chose snowboarding, and I went to the conventional bunny slope to begin my snow-skiing complementary lessons.

As the lessons progressed, the newbies were taught to bend forward and put one's skis inward when one wanted to stop. I had ridden horses quite a bit before my traumatic horse ride (in another story) and I was familiar with the pulling back motion of the reins when one wanted to stop the horse.

As I began to gain speed on the beginner slope, the ski instructor kept telling me to bend forward to stop. This bending forward motion, instead of bending backward to stop, seemed counterintuitive to me.

I, therefore, kept bending backward to stop and the law of physics made me go faster instead of slower. The faster I went, the more I bent backward. I just couldn't seem to go against all that horse-riding pulling-back-on-the reins wisdom and would end up screaming for the ski instructor's help.

After many attempts, the exasperated ski instructor finally told me to just fall down every time I wanted to stop. So, I did. Ski, splat! Ski, splat! Ski, splat!

With every fall, I had to pull myself up. The fun of snow-skiing decreased in exact proportion with each clown fall splat.

In the end, my daughter had a great time snowboarding with the younger adult set, and I spent the rest of the time recovering in the tour bus. Although I never went skiing again, I understand that all the pratfalls were hilarious to watch.

LIFE LESSON: WHEN THINGS GET DANGEROUS, KNOW HOW TO STOP.

A NEW FASHION

WHEN I FIRST BEGAN TEACHING ELEMENTARY SCHOOL IN THE 80'S, the dress code was very different. Women were expected to wear skirts or dresses (no slacks or pants) and wear shoes that did not show any toes.

As a result, most teachers wore pantyhose and pumps to work. I had bought the same style of pumps, but in three different colors to comply with the current dress code. Thus, I purchased a black pair, a navy pair, and a beige pair of pumps as these colors would hopefully coordinate with my outfits.

At the time, I was participating in a leadership internship at my school and one of the duties was to be present when the first busses arrived around 6:30 am. (The rural school had to make several runs, so school personnel were required to be there early to greet the busses. I was assigned that duty.)

I greeted the students and escorted them to the cafeteria where the students would wait until the classes began.

In the winter months, it was still dark in the mornings when the busses would arrive. On one of these winter mornings, I was greeting the students as usual.

After my duty was finished, I proceeded to my fourth-grade class and taught the entire day, walking around my students, presenting information at the front of the class, and escorting the students to/from lunch/recess and specials. A regular day – except for one tiny thing.

At the end of the day when students were packing up to go home, I happened to glance down at my feet, and I was shocked and embarrassed to discover that I was wearing one black shoe and one navy blue shoe. (Apparently, I had not noticed since it was dark when I arrived at school and when I left my home.)

I looked up and asked the class why no one had mentioned this fashion faux pas to me (I could have gone home at lunch, at least, to correct the error!) and a student sincerely said, "Ms. Hogi, we thought you were starting a new fashion."

I have checked my shoes every day since then.

LIFE LESSON: SMALL THINGS CAN MAKE A BIG DIFFEENCE.

BOO BOO'S BOO BOO

MY BEST FRIEND, MICHELLE, HAS A MINIATURE CHIHUAHUA NAMED Boo Boo.

As a puppy, Boo Boo was very tiny and could get into many places that larger breed dog puppies could not navigate.

It was my first-time meeting Boo Boo when I flew out to visit my friend in New Mexico during spring break. Michelle had carefully warned me to keep my suitcase closed so little Boo Boo could not get inside and take things, as apparently, the little puppy liked to find new items and carry then off in her mouth. Thus, I carefully closed my suitcase every time I used it.

After a fun time with my friend, the spring break ended, and I returned to New Jersey. I received a call the next day from my friend Michelle who relayed this story:

She had awakened in the morning thinking she had gone blind as when she opened her eyes, it was still dark. As she got up, she realized that a pair of underwear had been placed on her face while she was sleeping. It was a pair of my underwear!

Somehow, Boo Boo had gotten into my suitcase and ran off with a pair of my underwear. As my friend, Michelle, had slept, Boo Boo waited to reward Michelle by giving her her latest treasure – my underwear. Boo Boo had, therefore, carefully placed my underwear on Michelle's face.

Laughing, my friend, Michelle, told me she would wash the pair of underwear and send it in the mail back to New Jersey.

Days later, I opened my package from New Mexico to reveal my freshly cleaned pair of underwear – returned home again, via Boo Boo.

LIFE LESSON: SOMETIMES THINGS CAN COME BACK TO YOU.

BOO BOO DID WHAT?

MY BEST FRIEND, MICHELLE, HAS A MINIATURE CHIHUAHUA NAMED Boo Boo. Boo Boo is a very curious and intelligent dog. My friend had wanted to take Boo Boo for her first walk in her neighborhood. Here is what happened, as told by Michelle:

Boo Boo and Michelle were having a nice walk in the neighborhood. They were walking on the sidewalk on their way to a local neighborhood park.

Suddenly, a house door burst open, and a large male guard dog burst forth and ran toward Boo Boo. Michelle thought that this would be the end of Boo Boo as little Boo Boo looked like a single serving size to the large male dog.

As my friend, Michelle, watched in horror, the barking and menacing dog approached Boo Boo, and, surprisingly, Boo Boo remained calm. When the male guard dog lurched toward her, Boo Boo simply jumped up and bit down on one of the male dog's hanging private parts.

Boo Boo, literally, held on to the dog in this manner, and the large dog took off running with Boo Boo attached. As the male dog ran off, Boo Boo held on tightly and swung back and forth while the large dog galloped down the street.

Michelle ran after the dogs in pursuit.

She finally caught up with both dogs in the neighborhood park. The large dog had laid down on the ground and Boo Boo was still attached. Michelle gingerly detached Boo Boo from the large dog's private part and the large dog's owner returned the dog to his home.

The large dog never attacked Boo Boo again.

LIFE LESSON: STAY CALM IN AN EMERGENCY.

PLEASE TAKE A SEAT

WHEN I WAS TEACHING OVERSEAS, I HAD THE OPPORTUNITY TO travel. My mom and friends, who had belonged to a grief group, were in their second year of recovery. As part of their recovery, they had all decided to travel to Spain as one of the members spoke fluent Spanish. Since I was already overseas, the trip was coordinated with my spring break so I would have the week to join them in their adventure.

This is how I found myself traveling over the Iraqi airspace on my way to Spain (via Amsterdam) on the day in March 2003 when the United States invaded Iraq. (However, that is another story.)

Upon my arrival onto the Spanish Mediterranean coast, I noticed that I had started to feel rundown and had the beginning of a cold.

As I walked along the beach walk, I noticed a restaurant was selling freshly squeezed orange juice. Voilà! *That would help with my cold symptoms,* I thought. I asked the hostess if I were able to have some orange juice to go. She graciously agreed and asked me to take a seat in one of the chairs in the waiting area.

After paying, I sat down and waited for the juice. When it was ready, I stood up to retrieve the orange juice.

I was shocked to discover that the white chair was somehow attached to my bottom – it was literally part of my body now! I had, truly, *taken* a seat!

I attempted to pull it off me, however, I was overcome with laughter at my predicament. Guests in the restaurant were wildly laughing as well. The hostess did her best to dislodge the chair off my bottom, however, this attempt was not successful. This new development only added to the hilarity.

The hostess then went to get help from the chef. A big, burly man appeared and pulled hard on the chair. A vacuum release sound was heard, and I was finally dislodged from the chair!

The guests in the restaurant then all clapped, and I, good-naturedly, took a bow, grabbed my juice, and walked off.

It was hard to drink the juice, though, as I couldn't stop laughing.

LIFE LESSON: LEARN TO LAUGH AT YOURSELF.

SHE WENT BY IN A FLASH

IT WAS A HOT AND HUMID DAY IN MAY AS I PARKED MY CAR IN THE school faculty parking lot. The parents were lined up in their cars for the morning drop-off so their children could attend the elementary school. Being a teacher, I strode across the parking lot on my way to enter the building and go to work.

I heard several horns honking and all the honking was disturbing. My thought was, *How rude. I wish these people would be more polite.*

As I continued to walk onto the sidewalk to enter the school doors, I heard a voice cry out in the wilderness, "Ms. Hogi, your dress is up in the back!"

To my utter dismay, I felt behind my dress, and sure enough, my dress somehow was hiked up high and I had exposed my underwear. On my walk across the school parking lot, during the busiest drop-off time, I had managed to flash every parent and student in a car!

I immediately pulled down my dress and quickly remedied the situation.

I told the staff that I needed to take a Humiliation Day as I had just flashed the school community in the parking lot. Unfortunately, such a day did not exist.

I somehow pulled myself together (literally and emotionally) and proceeded teaching my students that day.

I later realized that all that horn honking in the morning had been directed at me – not out of rudeness, but out of an attempt to alert me that my dress was up in the back.

To this day, I have no idea who yelled at me in the parking lot. I am just grateful that they did.

LIFE LESSON: DETAILS CAN BE VERY IMPORTANT.

COURAGEOUS STORIES

Courage is found in unlikely places.
—J.R.R. Tolkien

A FLYING LEAP

When I was a pre-teen, I wanted a horse. My paternal grandparents had a ranch and both of my maternal cousins, who lived locally, had their own horses. I wanted one, too. However, no amount of begging and pleading could sway my parent's minds.

Then, one of my good friends in junior high (9th grade) got a retired racehorse for her birthday. She invited me to go riding with her.

My parents weren't crazy about this idea, either. I reassured them that we would be riding, double backed, at the junior high fields which were close by. Perfectly safe.

At last, they consented, and I met my girlfriend, and horse, to go riding.

She put the bit in the horse's mouth, and then the blanket on the back of the horse, and the saddle on top of that. The plan was for her to sit in the saddle, and I would sit behind the saddle, bareback, and hold on to her.

So, once the horse was ready to go, she climbed up onto the saddle, and I climbed onto the bare rear end of the horse. Since we were both in position, she kicked the horse hard with her feet. The horse took off into a full gallop with such force (it was a racehorse, after all) that my friend dropped the reins of the horse.

The horse, in a full gallop, and with free rein, (as my friend was no longer holding onto the reins), was given its *head* which means in horse racing parlance, to now run as fast as it possibly could run. Although it was a retired racehorse, it was still very young and could gallop really fast.

It was galloping so fast that in no time, we were on the edge of the field and were quickly approaching a long wire from a telephone pole angled and attached to the ground.

We had both started screaming as we were here headed straight for that wire.

At the very last moment, the horse did an almost 90-degree turn, and we somehow still held on. We were still screaming, though, as the run-a-away horse was now galloping full out on the streets of the nearby neighborhood. Cars were swerving, dogs were barking, and we continued to scream and do our best to hold on.

To complicate matters more, though, my friend had not pulled the strap on the horse's saddle tightly enough and, with the shifting weight of the 90-degree turn, the saddle was slowly sliding off the back of the horse.

However, the back of the horse was exactly where I was sitting, holding on for dear life, to my friend. So now, I was faced with a huge problem. I began to feel the saddle sliding off the back and I could see the galloping horse's hooves getting closer and closer to my body.

To save myself from a severe injury or worse, I decided that I would have to fling myself off the horse and, hopefully, land in someone's grassy front yard.

I flung myself off the horse with all my might.

Unfortunately, I had forgotten that I had put my right foot through the right stirrup to not fall off the backside. Not having a clear foot prevented me from reaching a grassy front yard.

I landed on the sidewalk on my head, apparently, and

passed out. I later learned that my friend, once I had leapt, had simply slid off the backside of the horse, still in the saddle, and landed unceremoniously in the street. Thankfully, she was unhurt.

As for me? I opened my eyes and noticed I was in someone's living room and (this is fuzzy) somehow ended up at the hospital emergency room.

I had a huge bump on my head and my entire right leg was swollen and hurt a lot. I had to use crutches for many weeks and my hair fell out over the bump area. All of this was so traumatic that I became afraid of horses. I still am.

LIFE LESSON: SOMETIMES IT IS IMPORTANT TO HANG ON FOR AS LONG AS YOU CAN.

A SONG OF COURAGE

THE STUDENT PEOPLE-TO-PEOPLE PROGRAM, THAT I WAS privileged to be a part of during the summer of 1970, included a visit to the then Soviet Union. Our group was to be the first American tour group since the Cold War began.

After flying from California to the East Coast, all the student ambassadors were briefed by the United States State Department. We were told not to sell anything to the Russian people. We were also told that we would most likely be followed and watched the entire time we were in Moscow and in Leningrad.

Growing up in northern California, where I had atomic bomb drills in my elementary school because of our "enemy," the Soviet Union, it was not a stretch to say I was quite nervous entering enemy territory on this trip. The briefing from the United States State Department did not soothe my growing anxiety.

After many experiences touring with the Communist tour guides, meeting Russian students, getting sick on the food, trying to live like an ordinary Russian on $3 a day, and hearing and seeing much propaganda, I was more than ready to go on to Finland. I was craving fresh fruit and vegetables and smiling people.

As our group of teenage ambassadors entered the Leningrad Airport, we were met by a Russian security detail. My guess is that they had been instructed to detain us and thoroughly check our luggage to ensure that nothing left the country that the Russian government didn't want anyone to see back in the United States.

Whatever the reason, we were all detained in a room with no food, bathroom facilities, or an explanation.

Looking out a window, we watched our plane fly off. The teacher-leaders, who were our chaperones, were very concerned for our safety and well-being.

One of the student ambassadors had a guitar and that student started playing the guitar and singing the song,

"Leaving on a Jet Plane" as one of the lyrics was "Don't know when I'll be back again."

Emboldened by this song, our group started to compose new lyrics to the song. We named the new song, "Stuck in Leningrad." It was a defiant song and we kept singing it over and over and louder and louder. We had memorized the words and singing the protest song gave us courage and hope.

It is my guess that our song could be heard in the airport main venue, and it must have been a nuisance to the Russian security detail.

After hours had passed, and with no explanation, we were all released and boarded a different plane to Finland. Some of us cried and laughed in relief when we finally landed in Helsinki.

Apparently, the Cold War was still in effect.

LIFE LESSON: IN A LOUD VOICE, PROTEST AGAINST INJUSTICE.

SHE WENT THUMP

As a single parent, I rarely had an opportunity to have a vacation. However, there was onetime when I could share a quick getaway to Cancun, Mexico, with my then boyfriend, so I was on my way.

One of the activities was a tour of Chichen-Itza, an archaeological historical site of Mayan buildings. One of the structures of note was a step pyramid that was constructed for ritual sacrifice/worship named El Castillo. It had 91 small steps to the top of each side, plus the bottom.

At the time, one could climb up the pyramid. My boyfriend wanted to climb to the top and I carefully climbed up the steps as well.

As I turned around to enjoy the panoramic view, I had a strange sensation pulse through my body. My heart throbbed and by body went limp and I started to shake. I immediately sat down. (I had yet to have the Eye of the Needle experience.) I did not know that I had a fear of heights and that this fear had temporarily paralyzed me.

After catching my breath, it occurred to me that I must be afraid of being up so high. I had flown on planes, I had hiked in the mountains, and I had been to the top of the Eiffel Tower, so I struggled to make sense of what was happening to me.

Although I did not understand it, all I knew is that my body refused to move. The tour bus driver started to honk the horn of the tour bus to gather the tourists as it was time to leave.

My boyfriend, who was not known for his patience, implored me to get up and get going. I told him that I couldn't move. Frustrated, he reminded me that there were no helicopters that were going to come and rescue me.

I still couldn't stand up, so I asked him to hold my hand.

So, in a sitting position, I thumped down the pyramid, one step at a time, sitting on my backside. Thump. Thump. Thump. I went down all 91 steps on that side of the pyramid sitting down.

Using this method, I was able to get to the bottom of the pyramid and get on the tour bus and return safely to Cancun. Speaking of bottoms, yes, I had a very sore one.

LIFE LESSON: SOMETIMES IT IS IMPORTANT TO TAKE ONE STEP AT A TIME.

THE EYE OF
THE NEEDLE

AFTER I SAW THE MOVIE, *THE LAST OF THE MOHICANS,* I WAS mesmerized by the music and story line. When I finished up all the presentations and was on my way home from a conference in the North Carolina mountains, I had the opportunity to visit the location of the filming of the movie.

I entered the park late and I had only a couple of hours before the park would close. I wanted to get to the place where the cliff scene was filmed, and I didn't have the time to walk the longer route.

I saw a trail sign that said, "The Eye of the Needle," and it gave the liability warning that this trail was for experienced climbers. I thought to myself that, *A nature trail climb couldn't be that hard,* and off I went on this shortcut.

I reached the Eye of the Needle and there appeared to be an opening to the inside of a long vertical rock. I went inside the entrance, and it was immediately dark and confining.

There was a metal ladder that was vertical, and it went straight up into the darkness. Water dripped on the rungs so that they were very slippery. One would have to navigate the slippery steps in the dark to advance on this trail.

Suddenly, my body went limp, and I felt paralyzed. I couldn't move. I didn't understand what was happening to me, however, this same feeling had happened to me in Chichen-Itza with a fear of heights. A total fear engulfed my very being. I started to cry, and I couldn't seem to move up the ladder or return to the outside of the rock.

Unbeknownst to me, I had just discovered that I was also very claustrophobic. The horrifying thought occurred to me that no one could hear me if I cried out for help. As this even happened before cell phones were invented, I had no way of communicating to the outside world that I was trapped inside the Eye of the Needle. No wonder that the unofficial trail rule is to hike with a buddy!

In my despair, I was left with the realization that I had to depend on my myself to solve the problem.

I tried to approach the ladder. My heart was throbbing, and I felt like my body was moving through heavy cement. Slowly, I grabbed the sides of the metal ladder and pulled myself onto the first rung. Cautiously, carefully, I gradually worked my way up the ladder, one rung at a time.

My entire body was shaking as I finally reached the open portal at the top of the rock. I pulled myself into the fresh air. I just laid on my back to get my feelings, both physical and emotional, under control.

After slowly rising from the prone position, I walked to the cliff view and reached my goal. The scene was truly beautiful.

I walked the long trail on my return to the parking lot and gift store. I bought a souvenir from the gift store as I wanted to remember this pivotal day in my life – the day when I had to find the courage to face my fears and to move on and upward.

LIFE LESSON: FACE YOUR FEARS.

A ROCKY EXPERIENCE

ONE OF MY LIFE'S WISHES WAS TO VISIT THE GIZA PYRAMIDS IN
Egypt. I had the opportunity to have my lifelong dream come
true during a winter vacation while I was living overseas. I
had arranged for my adult son and adult daughter to join me
on their short winter school break.

We met at the Cairo Airport and settled in. We were
going to visit the pyramids!

On the tour day, we could see low-lying fog on top of the
pyramids when we first viewed them from our tour bus. As
the tour bus parked, we disembarked and saw this wonder
of the ancient world as the fog began to dissipate. The view
was truly breathtaking.

Our tour guide informed us that there was an opportunity
to go inside the large pyramid, however, there was a limit on

the number of visitors who would be allowed to go inside. As the rest of the fog cleared, we waited in a special line to get tickets to enter the pyramid.

Although the wait was long, we were so excited to get three tickets to enter the pyramid.

As we entered, there was a large, illuminated entrance and my thought was that this inside tour was going to be very doable. Due to the Eye of the Needle experience (another story in this book), I knew I was claustrophobic – however, the entrance was not dark or enclosed. I felt satisfied that this experience was going to go well.

When we walked around a turn, though, things drastically changed. The pathway had turned into a steep climb through a darkened narrow tunnel. My claustrophobic fear began to overtake me. I stopped in my tracks. My son went in, and my daughter tried to encourage me. She told me that this was a "once in-a-lifetime-experience."

A young child passed me and entered the tunnel. I thought that if a small child could enter the tunnel, then certainly I could be able to enter the tunnel as well. I gathered all the courage I could muster, and I made my decision. I was going to do this.

Slumping over to fit into the narrow tunnel, I pushed

myself to put one step in front of another. After a reasonable amount of time, the tunnel stopped, and I could stand up. Then, another tunnel to enter the King's Chamber. I had to muster my courage again to continue.

As I entered the King's Chamber, I was momentarily thrilled that I had made it! However, it then occurred to me, much to my horror, that I had to go back out the same way I had come, and I had to return, again, through the pyramid.

When leaving the King's Chamber, I held on to my adult children and took baby steps all the way back through the tunnels.

At long last, we returned to the wide, lit trail that led out of the pyramid. Once into the fresh air and sunlight, I lifted my hands into the air and did a Rocky celebration. I had survived being inside a pyramid!

LIFE LESSON: SOMETIMES YOU MUST GO THROUGH DARKNESS BEFORE YOU CAN SEE THE LIGHT.

SEE YOU AROUND THE BEND: A BONUS STORY

(Note: I told this story on Valentine's Day)

I WAS IN PRESCHOOL WHEN I FIRST FELL IN LOVE WITH MES. I SAW him in my preschool Sunday School class. It was love at first sight. I just knew that someday I would grow up and marry MES. I only saw him once a week on Sundays, however, I looked forward to seeing MES every time.

Imagine my happiness when I transferred to a different K-8 elementary school and discovered that he also attended this school! There was only one class for every grade, so he was in my class. I now got to see him every day, except Saturdays. True bliss.

Life was good. All my classmates knew how much we liked each other. As the years passed, we could be seen playing together and talking together a lot of the time.

Then, sixth grade happened. My beloved MES told me that his father was going to start a new job in the state of Washington, and he would be moving. What? NOOOOOOOOOOOOOOO!!!

He told me, before he moved, that he would come and get me in northern California, and we would attend college together in Washington.

He moved away and I was miserable.

I really didn't have another boyfriend until I turned 16. No one seemed to be at the level of my MES.

Eventually, I got married (see story about Hi, Ho, Silver, Away!) at 18 and moved to Cupertino, California in September.

I had just returned from the Hawaiian honeymoon when a strange car pulled up in front of the house in Cupertino, California. Out stepped a tall young man who looked like the grown-up version of MES. IT WAS MES!

He had kept his promise from the sixth grade and had driven down from the state of Washington to my parent's house in northern California. He was then directed to my new location.

I was absolutely stunned. Had I received even one letter or phone call in those six years, I would have waited for my beloved MES's return.

I didn't know what to do, so I just thanked him for finding me. Then, he left.

I eventually divorced my first husband. I then located MES in Washington state. When I found him, he had since married. So, I went on my way again.

I got married a second time. MES divorced his first wife and found me in Texas. However, since I was married again, he went on his way.

I then divorced my second husband and went on my way.

In 1991, I received an invitation to attend a celebration reunion of all students who attended our K-8 school in northern California. It had closed in 1978, and the reunion committee had wanted all the faculty/staff/students who had attended the school to get together one last time.

I had been asked by a classmate if I knew where MES were living as no one knew where he was at the time. I told the organizers that I would find him. Years and years before the Internet and cell phones, I was able to locate a family member of his and I was thus able to find out that he was working in Japan. I passed on the information to the organizers.

At last! A reunion of the two of us. I, technically, had a boyfriend (who I later found out was married – unbeknownst to me – however, that is another story) but we were both single at the same time. I flew to California from the East Coast, and he flew to California from Japan.

At long last! I was so happy to see him! All my classmates were betting that we would now get married. He looked as handsome as I remembered him.

While we talked, it became clear that he was very committed to his life in Japan, and I was very committed to my life on the East Coast.

We had missed our chance in this lifetime.

As he walked me to my rental car after the event, he gave me a goodbye kiss – my first kiss from MES. As we kissed, a meteor streaked across the starlit sky.

We committed to being together in the next lifetime and his last words to me before I drove off in tears were, "See you around the bend."

I hope to keep that promise.

LIFE LESSON: BELIEVE IN HAPPILY EVER AFTERS.

LIFE LESSONS SUMMARY

Humorous Stories

1. The Bunny Trap

   - *LIFE CAN BE FULL OF SURPRISES.*

2. My Best Mermaid Impression

   - *SOMETIMES IT IS IMPORTANT TO LET GO.*

3. An American in Paris

   - *THINGS CAN BE DIFFERENT FROM WHAT THEY APPEAR.*

4. Hi, Ho, Silver, Away!

   • *HELP MAY COME WHEN YOU LEAST EXPECT IT.*

5. Splat!

   • *WHEN THINGS GET DANGEROUS, KNOW HOW TO STOP.*

6. A New Fashion

   • *SMALL THINGS CAN MAKE A BIG DIFFERENCE.*

7. Boo Boo's Boo Boo

   • *SOMETIMES THINGS CAN COME BACK TO YOU.*

8. Boo Boo Did What?

   • *STAY CALM IN AN EMERGENCY.*

9. Please Take a Seat

   • *LEARN TO LAUGH AT YOURSELF.*

10. She Went by in a Flash

- *DETAILS CAN BE VERY IMPORTANT.*

Courageous Stories

11. A Flying Leap

- *SOMETIMES IT IS IMPORTANT TO HANG ON FOR AS LONG AS YOU CAN.*

12. A Song of Courage

- *IN A LOUD VOICE, PROTEST AGAINST INJUSTICE.*

13. She Went Thump

- *SOMETIMES IT IS IMPORTANT TO TAKE ONE STEP AT A TIME.*

14. The Eye of the Needle

- *FACE YOUR FEARS.*

15. A Rocky Experience

- *SOMETIMES YOU MUST GO THROUGH DARKNESS BEFORE YOU SEE THE LIGHT.*

16. See You Around the Bend: A Bonus Story

- *BELIEVE IN HAPPILY EVER AFTERS.*

Lightning Source UK Ltd.
Milton Keynes UK
UKHW040301181121
394157UK00010B/458/J